INTRODUCTION

'Had a look round the ship (didn't take long by the way). I am more accustomed to small ships but this beats anything I've been in. The decks are bare iron. We have one funnel and two boilers and I am glad to see we burn oil fuel … at any rate we'll coal ship through a hose.'

Diary of Leading Signalman Henry Mulligan, June 1915

The 'monitor' HMS *M.33* is a small ship with a big history. Built with incredible speed in 1915, she is one of only three surviving Royal Navy warships of the First World War, and the only remaining fighting veteran of that year's bloody Gallipoli Campaign. *M.33* offers the unique opportunity to see how men lived and fought in small ships 100 years ago, and to understand a little of the dangers they faced, floating in a basic steel box in shallow waters underneath Turkish guns.

HMS *M.33* is also a ship with a long history of service and of restoration. Until her final sale by the Navy in 1987 she had served not only as a monitor but had been adapted to be a minelayer, a workshop and a hulk. She was known as *M.33*, HMS *Minerva*, *C.23* and RMAS *Minerva* – and was even painted with the unofficial name HMS '*Mugwump*' for three months.

Now finally, after sterling work by Hampshire County Council to rescue and conserve the ship since 1990, the National Museum of the Royal Navy is delighted to complete the job, to open the ship to visitors and use her to commemorate the Gallipoli Campaign.

DESIGNING AND BUILDING *M.33*

'In accordance with your directions … an outline sketch for the Light Draft Gunboat carrying two 6-inch guns is forwarded herewith.'
Letter from Charles Lillicrap, 12 March 1915

On 15 March 1915 the Admiralty ordered the construction of five new monitors; the last of these was to become HMS *M.33*. Monitors were designed to carry heavy guns but with a shallow draft that enabled them to get close to shore and bombard land targets. They were simple, cheap and quick to build – and were very much a ship of their time.

At the start of the war three river-monitors, built for the Brazilian Navy but requisitioned by the Royal Navy before their delivery, had proved their worth off the Belgian coast, using their guns against German forces trying to seize Channel ports. Winston Churchill as First Lord of the Admiralty – always looking for ships that could be used (and risked) in offensive amphibious operations (perhaps in the North Sea, perhaps in the Baltic) – quickly ordered the monitors *M.1–M.14*. Another 14 monitors with a single, smaller 9.2-inch gun – *M.15–M.28* – were then ordered in February 1915. These monitors varied considerably in their size and the power of their guns; the largest, like HMS *M.13* (which became HMS *Marshal Ney*), carried two mighty 15-inch guns and weighed over 6,500 tons, dwarfing little *M.33*. However, apart from sharing the same basic purpose, the monitors were all united by the most important factor in their design and construction – the availability of guns.

As First Lord of the Admiralty Churchill requisitioned or ordered many monitors. The monitors *M.1–M.14* carried large 12-, 14- or 15-inch guns; as large ships it was felt they must have names and were quickly re-christened; the monitors with smaller guns like *M.33* only ever used a number.

M.33 and her four sisters were designed because trials of the new *Queen Elizabeth*-class battleships from January 1915 showed that their secondary armament of four 6-inch guns was too near the waterline to be used at sea; after two were re-sited higher up this still left a total of ten spare. In early March, using the design for *M.15–M.28* as a starting point, Assistant Constructor Charles Lillicrap worked out a simple plan for five monitors to carry two guns each. The ships were ordered from Harland and Wolff in Belfast, but construction of *M.32* and *M.33* was subcontracted to Workman, Clark and Co. (known as 'the wee yard' but still employing over 9,000 workers). Construction was amazingly quick: the keel was laid on 1 April; the ship was launched on 22 May; and the crew joined on 17 June.

Just four months after work started, *M.33* was off the Turkish coast, ready to take part in the Gallipoli Campaign.

These images from Harland and Wolff show the stages of the amazingly rapid construction of *M.33*'s sisters, *M.29*, *M.30* and *M.31*.

THE GALLIPOLI CAMPAIGN

'Is there no alternative to sending our men to chew barbed wire in Flanders …'
Winston Churchill, First Lord of the Admiralty, 1915

The Dardanelles Straits.

By the end of 1914 Allied forces had suffered terrible casualties, and fighting on the Western Front had reached stalemate. It was in this environment that on 13 January 1915 Winston Churchill was able to persuade other, less focused political and military leaders in the War Council to approve the preparation of a naval expedition, 'to invade and take the Gallipoli Peninsula with Constantinople as its objective'. The half-formed plan, that won approval against the advice of Churchill's naval professionals, aimed to knock Turkey (allied with Germany since November 1914) out of the war. The reasoning was that an invasion would relieve pressure on Britain's ally Russia, and thereby strengthen the Eastern Front and ultimately weaken Germany.

The expedition began in February with a joint British and French fleet bombarding the forts at the entrance to the Dardanelles – the narrow seaway which led to the Turkish capital and the Black Sea. Then on 18 March the ships made their attempt to rush and 'Force the Narrows', but this was aborted following the loss of one French and two British battleships to mines and artillery fire. After debate it was agreed not to retry until the Army could gather its forces to land, capture the high ground behind the Turkish Forts – which was predicted to be a swift operation – and so allow the Navy unhindered progress.

The Allied forces that were assembled numbered five divisions, including the Australian and New Zealand Army Corps (ANZAC). The doomed landings eventually took place on 25 April across five beaches round the Gallipoli Peninsula. It is impossible here to do justice to the heroism or to the chaos of the landings, the desperate attempts to advance, or to the offensives and counter-offensives which resolved by June, with a tragic irony, into another bloody trench stalemate.

↑ A steam pinnace towing four boats for landings at Cape Helles, 25 April.

← Men of the Lancashire Fusiliers 42nd Division waiting to disembark.

↓ Sedd el Bahr Fort, a key part of the Turkish defences at the entrance to the Dardanelles, which also overlooked the landings on V Beach.

The Royal Navy was active throughout: landing troops; ensuring sufficient supplies reached the shore; evacuating casualties; and providing supporting gunfire. However, German U-boats posed a threat particularly to these bombarding ships, and when the 12,000-ton battleship HMS *Triumph* was torpedoed on 25 May, it became too risky to position such valuable ships permanently offshore.

In the knowledge of this stalemate HMS *M.33* – along with 13 other smaller monitors – received sailing orders for Gallipoli. With instructions to 'keep her light guns manned' and take 'every precaution against submarine attack', she left Pembroke Dockyard on 28 June. She departed proudly under her own steam, but was soon, rather ignominiously, taken in tow across the Bay of Biscay and all the way to Malta by the collier *Blackheath*.

M.33 AT GALLIPOLI

Turkish shell splash off the Peninsula. *M.33*'s shallow draft took the ship perilously close inshore.

'Same old noise and flare ups here every night. … Incessant musketry and machine gun fire, one or two stray bullets whizzed over our fo'c's'le. Anchored rather close inshore tonight.'
Diary of Leading Signalman Henry Mulligan, 10 August 1915

On 24 July *M.33* arrived in the Aegean Sea at the Allied base of Mudros on the Island of Lemnos, just 50 miles from the Gallipoli Peninsula. With barely a pause she was ordered to join the naval forces using their guns to support a final major offensive to break the deadlock.

The plan was that in the early evening of 6 August the ANZAC forces, now dug-in inland from their landing beach at Anzac Cove, would break out and seize the strategic peaks in the Sari Bair Range. They would be reinforced by 20,000 fresh British troops landed at a new site further north at Suvla Bay. During the afternoon *M.33* took up position four miles offshore to the south of Suvla Bay near the headland of Gabe Tepe and began firing.

M.33 fired at established gun batteries, at mobile guns which popped up in new positions each day, and at Turkish troops gathering inland; working with directions from other ships and occasionally from a signal station onshore, she fired 316 shells in just eight days – almost exhausting her ammunition. The Captain could not be sure of the real impact of all their work, writing, 'during the whole period … there was no-one spotting for the ship so I have no means of judging the effect of my fire on the enemy'. Leading Signalman Henry Mulligan's diary tells us he was more confident, writing, 'don't think Mr Turk likes the look of us', but also that he became exhausted by long hours of steaming: '… been 8 days bumping about off flank. No shelter there, each had about 36 hours sleep in 8 days. No bread for last 5 days. What a Life!'

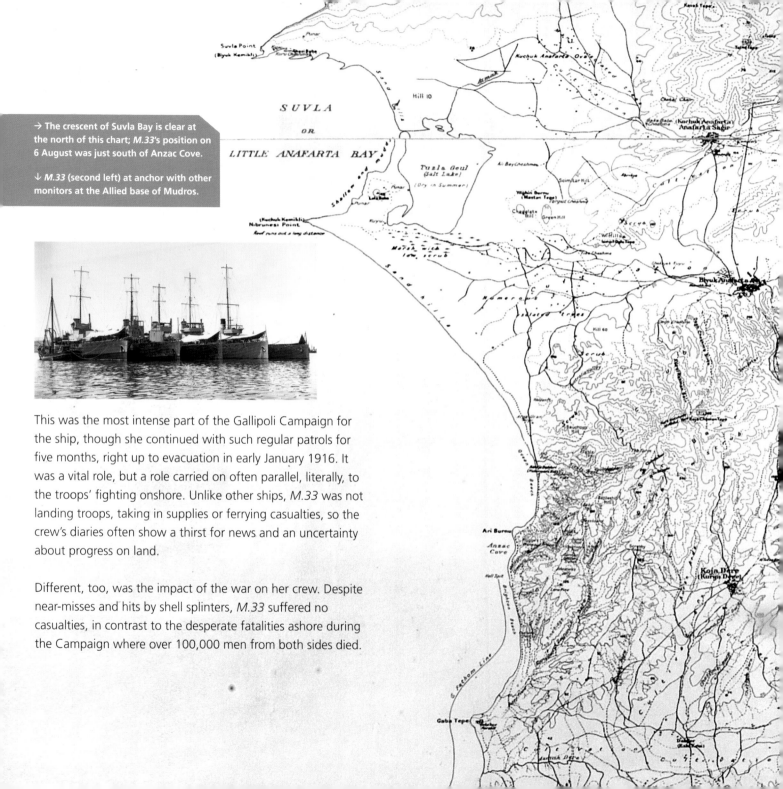

→ The crescent of Suvla Bay is clear at the north of this chart; *M.33*'s position on 6 August was just south of Anzac Cove.

↓ *M.33* (second left) at anchor with other monitors at the Allied base of Mudros.

This was the most intense part of the Gallipoli Campaign for the ship, though she continued with such regular patrols for five months, right up to evacuation in early January 1916. It was a vital role, but a role carried on often parallel, literally, to the troops' fighting onshore. Unlike other ships, *M.33* was not landing troops, taking in supplies or ferrying casualties, so the crew's diaries often show a thirst for news and an uncertainty about progress on land.

Different, too, was the impact of the war on her crew. Despite near-misses and hits by shell splinters, *M.33* suffered no casualties, in contrast to the desperate fatalities ashore during the Campaign where over 100,000 men from both sides died.

M.33 AFTER GALLIPOLI

'Went over to fire at a Turkish battery with one of our airplanes to spot for us, after she had circled around once or twice she was attacked by a Turkish FOKKER and got hit and had to come down but she managed to reach our ship and then fell in the water so we rescued 2 airmen and tied their machine up a stern and started to tow it but the dam Turks opened fired at us …'

Diary of Private Richard Chapple, RMLI, 6 November 1916

The withdrawal from Gallipoli did not mean the end of *M.33*'s service in the Aegean. For the best part of three years *M.33* was then part of Detached Squadrons, spread between the different Allied bases, seeking to control hundreds of miles of sea.

Just days after the final evacuation from the Peninsula on 8 January 1916, *M.33* steamed west to join the Bulgarian Campaign. For four months the ship was stationed at bases on either side of the Chalkidhikhi Peninsula – at Salonika in the east or at Stavros in the west. The front line extended well into neutral Greek territory, coming close to the sea, so there were limited opportunities for *M.33* to target shore positions. The rest of the time was spent protecting the bases, but not without risk. There were raids by aircraft and a Zeppelin (shot down) which dropped not just bombs but also metal darts, with the crew relying on the anti-aircraft gun mounted on the Funnel Deck – '… we were blazing away with our old 6 pounder as hard as we could'. In May 1916 the ship went south for six months to join the squadron blockading the Gulf of Smyrna on the Turkish coast. Over a busy period the crew witnessed the destruction of sister ship *M.30*, joined other monitors in shore bombardment and even took part in an attempt to steal some 2,000 Turkish cattle.

It is impossible here to detail the ship's service over the next two years, but it included vital work: watching for the German ships *Goeben* and *Breslau*; blockading ports; protecting bases; and harassing coastal shipping. The pattern of moving between different squadrons was established and included returns to the Gallipoli Peninsula – for another bombardment – to Stavros and to Smyrna; by 1918 it had become routine and almost monotonous.

↑ The crew painted *M.33* in early 1918 with this dazzle pattern, to confuse U-boats.

→ Not all these monitors were as lucky as *M.33*; *M.30* was hit, beached and burnt out on 15 May 1916.

As hostilities ceased in Bulgaria the original crew, who had joined the ship in June 1915, were finally replaced and the ship re-commissioned on 8 October 1918. The crew took passage to Bari in Italy and then travelled overland, arriving back at Devonport on Armistice Day, 1918. *M.33* herself stayed until February 1919, returning to Chatham on 10 April.

M.33 INTO NORTH RUSSIA

'While we are celebrating the conclusion of peace and our victory over Germany we must remember that the peace of mankind is still threatened by an even more sinister and brutal enemy whom we are fighting here.'

From a notice 'To be Read to All Ships' Companies on the Quarter-Deck 30th June 1919'

A month later *M.33* was off to war again: on 10 May 1919 she commissioned (this time with a Portsmouth crew) and steamed the next day to go and fight in support of 'White Russians' against revolutionary Bolshevik forces in the Russian Civil War. British military intervention in Russia had begun in June 1918. The initial aim was to hamper German forces by continuing the fighting on the Eastern Front, but for some, like Churchill – now Secretary of State for War – it became a way 'to strangle at birth the Bolshevik State'. A small British force had laid up over the winter of 1918 in Archangel in north Russia and *M.33* was sent as part of a major naval reinforcement.

M.33's journey took three weeks, rounding the North Cape to arrive at Archangel on 9 June. Here *M.33* became part of a naval force of approximately 20 vessels which within a few days headed up the Dvina River to spend three months

supporting forces ashore. Whilst at Gallipoli she had been dwarfed by battleships; on the Russian rivers, which needed a shallow draft, she was both more significant and her size more typical. The 'up river force' consisted of six other monitors (including her sister *M.31*), minesweepers, a seaplane carrier, repair ship, and coastal motor boats.

The months that followed were intense. Chief Engine Room Artificer Sydney Rutland wrote in his diary on 20 June: 'today has been one long roar, bang, whiz of shell fire from the monitors, land batteries and the enemy's batteries.' *M.33* took a full part in offensive actions and came under frequent attack. The ship was hit five times: the sea boat was broken to pieces; one shell smashed through the Wardroom; another penetrated the deck by the aft gun; and, most dramatically, an explosive shell came to rest in the Engine Room.

← DSM to Lieutenant Thomas Jones, RNR: 'Has displayed great coolness under fire and his accurate spotting aloft has been of great assistance. He has shown great zeal in preparing and perfecting the control and spotting instruments of this ship.' S.N.O. White Sea.

↙ *M.33*'s flotilla entering the White Sea – even in June there were still ice floes.

↓ This is the surviving repair from the damage of 7 August 1919. 'A projectile just under 6 inches diameter passed through the starboard side about six inches above the water-line, passed over the body of a Sergeant of Marines who was resting on the mess table as we fought in watch on watch. The projectile then turned for'ard through the Engine Room bulkhead and came to rest in the sump under the starboard engine, but did not explode.'

RISKS ON THE RIVER

'We now have dummy guns made of stove piping, blocks of wood etc. to represent our 6-inch and anti-aircraft guns which have been removed.'
Diary of Chief Engine Room Artificer Sydney Rutland, August 1919

For *M.33*, this summer on the north Russian rivers was very different and more perilous even than the summer spent at sea off Gallipoli.

In many ways it was an irregular campaign – the ships were intervening in a fluid civil war, marked by mutinies on both Russian sides. *M.33* operated without the huge logistical support that had been set up to move and supply hundreds of thousands of men at Gallipoli. Instead of a parallel existence off the coast, the crew was fully engaged with events ashore: at times the Marines landed to fight; at others men simply went to take a look at the enemy trenches. The crew also spent more time with local Russians, whether these were the peasants who came alongside to barter potatoes and milk, or the prisoners taken after significant fighting.

Fighting upriver brought unique risks. Not only were shore batteries and machine guns very close, but there were regular attacks from aircraft. Aside from what the crew called 'Bolo' (Bolshevik) gunboats, the enemy also floated explosive mines down the river, often disguised by brushwood. These caused significant ship losses on the river – the minesweepers HMS *Sword Dance* and HMS *Fandango* were both sunk within a few days of each other.

There were navigational risks also, especially when, at the end of August, water levels fell. As *M.33* prepared to steam back down the Dvina River, all efforts were made to lighten the ship, the Captain writing that, '… the guns and ammunition were got out. In fact everything that could be dispensed with for a few days, except for some rifles and a few cases of rations were discharged.' Even with these endeavours,

↑ Another monitor firing her for'ard gun, showing just how close the ships were to the river's banks.

← Chief Engine Room Artificer Sydney Rutland. Each 'war chevron' on his sleeve shows a year of overseas service in the First World War.

→ The ship's Captain, Lieutenant Commander K. Michell, was a submariner and seemed to revel in the irregularity of this campaign. He wrote in his memoir, 'Whilst upriver S.N.O.R seemed to get rather mixed up with all our numbers instead of names, so one evening I instructed the First Lieutenant to christen our ship "Mugwump" in six inch letters on the stern as an Aide Memoire. He asked me to give him instructions in writing as he did not like the idea.'

which gave a draft of less than 5 feet, the ship still grounded at some rapids. Desperate measures were called for but the Captain had a plan: 'I got [e]very spare man on to the quarter-deck holding something heavy, boxes of food, jugs of water, buckets of coal, ready for our passage, with our incomparable Sub Lieutenant preparing to make them jump together on the word, "Go!".' This unlikely method managed to move the ship, and *M.33* – albeit without any guns now as protection – got through. Other monitors did not make it; *M.25* and *M.27* had to be destroyed when aground.

The final withdrawal of British troops from Archangel took place on 27 September and *M.33* was amongst the very last of the Navy's ships to leave. Her luck had held again and after an uneventful return passage she docked at Chatham on 18 October.

INSIDE *M.33*

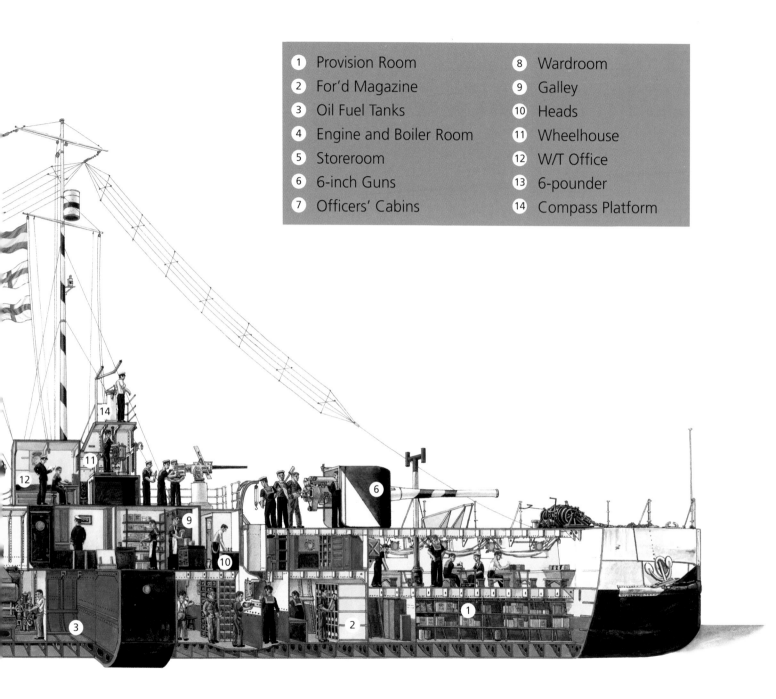

1. Provision Room
2. For'd Magazine
3. Oil Fuel Tanks
4. Engine and Boiler Room
5. Storeroom
6. 6-inch Guns
7. Officers' Cabins
8. Wardroom
9. Galley
10. Heads
11. Wheelhouse
12. W/T Office
13. 6-pounder
14. Compass Platform

THE SHIP'S COMPANY

H.M.S. M. Nº33.

'Captain and Officers inspected the ship. All hands on the fo'c's'le sang, "For he's a jolly good fellow". We all did our best to make things jolly and Christmas like. Each man had a drink from an officer.'
Diary of Leading Signalman Henry Mulligan, Christmas Day 1916

The 67 men and five officers who squeezed into *M.33*'s tiny steel hull in June 1915 came from very different backgrounds and brought with them varying levels of experience.

The Captain of the ship, Lieutenant-Commander Quintin Preston-Thomas, was a career officer who had joined as a 14-year-old cadet in 1894. However, the other four officers included: one young Medical Officer from the Royal Naval Volunteer Reserve; two Lieutenants from the Royal Naval Reserve (junior in rank but with years of experience from the Merchant Marine); and one commissioned Chief Gunner.

The crew were drawn from the Devonport Port Division meaning she was a 'West Country' ship. Many men did indeed come from Devon, Somerset and Gloucestershire, but others came from Ireland, Scotland, Wales, and across England. All were volunteers (conscription was not introduced until 1916), but they were a mixture of experienced reservists and men already signed on for a Navy career who served alongside those who signed for 'hostilities only'. The crew included men who in civilian life had been clerks, butchers, farmers and labourers, but who aboard ship might become Seamen, Stokers, Wireless Operators or Cook's Mates. The oldest at aged 50 had many decades of naval experience behind him; the youngest was just 16 and *M.33* was his first ship.

The crew that served in the First World War was away from home for nearly three and a half years, and though the officers did change as they were promoted or appointed to new duties, the crew was quite stable. The crew diaries

↖ This rare surviving cap tally from *M.33* belonged to Ordinary Seaman Sydney Hearn.

↑ *M.33* dressed for action, with splinter matting as protection round the Wheelhouse, and the crew's washing hung out along the starboard side.

→ With such a small crew very few photographs of the crew survive.

suggest they were a close-knit group, and if so this is fortunate because the ship was small enough to fit into an Admiralty Floating Dock and this meant that the crew did not get the leave that usually accompanied a return to the dockyard at Malta for regular refit and repair. In fact, the ship stayed in the Aegean for the whole of the war.

THE SHIP'S COMPANY

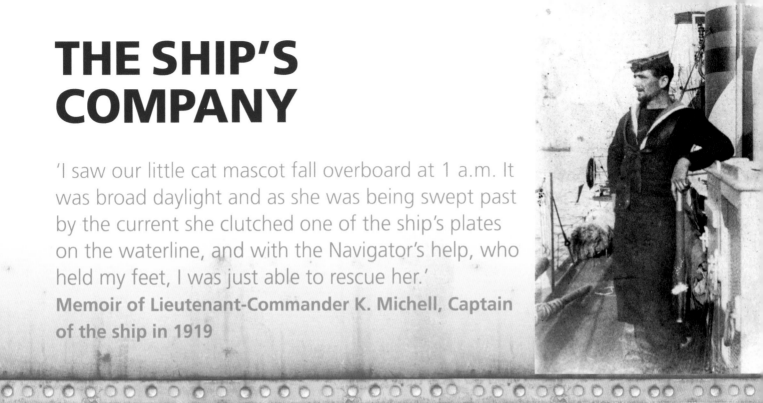

'I saw our little cat mascot fall overboard at 1 a.m. It was broad daylight and as she was being swept past by the current she clutched one of the ship's plates on the waterline, and with the Navigator's help, who held my feet, I was just able to rescue her.'

Memoir of Lieutenant-Commander K. Michell, Captain of the ship in 1919

Many years of research have given us a full picture of the lives of the crew, and some information has been gained from the men's surviving letters, diaries and memoirs – even at times from their descendants' stories. However, most details come from their official service records, and entries which show the times when they distinguished or perhaps disgraced themselves.

Coxswain, Beale who joined the ship in Belfast did not even reach Gallipoli, but was invalided at Malta in July 1915 with a gastric ulcer.

Boy Telegraphist, Norman Milburn the youngest crew member, born in 1899, aged 16 and was just 5' 5¾" when he joined the ship. He was a Shop Assistant from County Durham.

Fred Dockett, Private in the Royal Marine Light Infantry, who aged 41 received the Royal Humane Society's Bronze Medal, 'On the 31st October 1915, a seaman fell overboard from his ship at sea off the Gallipoli Peninsula, the night being dark … Dockett jumped in and kept him afloat until a boat reached them'.

John Culkin, Able Seaman of the Royal Fleet Reserve, born in 1876 who joined the Navy in 1894 and had the following tattoos, 'Letters, fouled anchor etc. on back of left hand and wrist, eagle on chest, rose on back of each hand'.

Reginald Brewer, Able Seaman who was 20 in 1915. He served in the ship for three years before being admitted to Yarmouth Naval Hospital as a 'dangerous lunatic' (he left a year later to the 'care of his mother').

↖ Leading Signalman Henry Mulligan was 27 at the start of the Campaign, already with nine years' service. His surviving diary gives a priceless picture of life aboard, from the viewpoint of an experienced naval hand.

↑ Royal Marine Private Richard Chapple, marked with a 'x' (front row). He was one of nine Marines on board, and also did duty as Officer's Steward.

→ Surgeon Probationer Edward Bilcliffe was the only Medical Officer on board. He was part of the RNVR, serving for the duration of hostilities only.

Other unofficial members of the crew, who left no records, include: dogs Nell and Squab, who served during the Gallipoli Campaign, and the cat 'Miss Miggins', who was a lucky mascot but sadly also a casualty in north Russia.

LIVING ON BOARD *M.33*

'There the Captain shot a wild boar in the water and we picked it up and the ship's company ate it.'
Diary of Private Richard Chapple, RMLI, 17 January 1916

The crew ashore with Nell, one of the ship's dogs.

Everyone on board lived close together in basic conditions. On the Upper Deck there were separate but tiny messes for the Chief Petty Officers and Stewards, and a Wardroom and six small cabins for the officers (two for the Captain). In practice these were not luxurious: a Surgeon's report states: 'the only method of egress is by the door on the port side … which when this is the weather side in a seaway renders the whole quarters liable to be flooded out by a sea coming over when the door is opened.'

The men's Mess Deck under the fo'c's'le, beneath the for'ard gun, was the space for 44 men to sling hammocks and 52 to eat their meals. When crammed full of the men's boots, ditty boxes, lifebelts, plates, tables and benches there was not an inch to spare, but even this was better than the conditions aft in the Steerage Flat where up to nine Marines lived. This was described as 'the worst feature in the ship … unsuitable from the point of view of ventilation and also the extreme dampness caused by the steam issuing from the steering engine. When underway there are the added discomforts of the noise and smell from the engine.'

In summer the heat on board was intense; despite temporary awnings to give shade, the ship's bare steel quickly heated up and spaces like the Mess Deck and Engine Room were stifling. Cold was also a problem, for example in the bitterly cold storms which hit Gallipoli in November 1915. The only heating on board came from a single electrical fire in the officers' Wardroom and a heating stove on the Mess Deck. A Surgeon on a sister ship wrote that, 'during the cold weather the sweating of the sides and deck above is very great, so much so that the men have to fix oil skins over their hammocks to prevent the dripping'.

← The Mess Deck where 44 men slept in hammocks and 52 ate their meals.

→ The 'heads'. There were just two toilets and two wash basins for the crew.

↓ The Galley, with a coal-fired oven which cooked food for both officers and men.

Such a small, cheaply built ship was not designed to be self-sufficient. It lacked many facilities such as a separate Sick Berth, or refrigerator, which were common on larger ships. Instead it relied on large old cruisers as base ships – for the Gallipoli Campaign this was HMS *Europa* at Mudros and for north Russia it was HMS *Fox* at Archangel. Throughout the three and a half years *M.33* was in the Mediterranean, Mudros was extremely important. It offered the chance to buy fresh provisions such as eggs, onions, cucumbers, apples, pears, melons, walnuts and figs. It also provided time ashore and the opportunity for frequent football, polo and swimming matches with other ships – even for boxing contests on the fo'c's'le.

POWERING
M.33

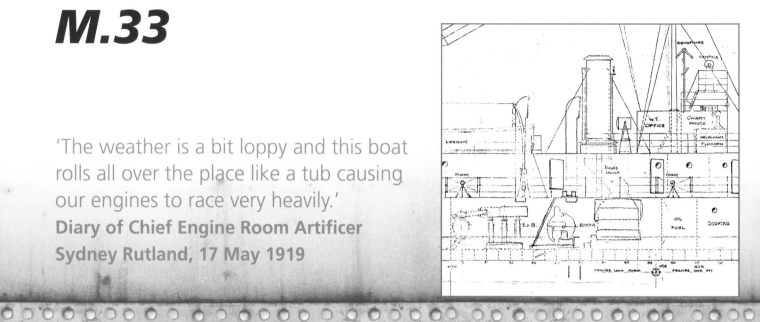

'The weather is a bit loppy and this boat rolls all over the place like a tub causing our engines to race very heavily.'
Diary of Chief Engine Room Artificer Sydney Rutland, 17 May 1919

M.33's double-height Engine Room contained twin-screw triple-expansion engines which generated 400ihp. These were adequate for the ship's purpose, but hardly made her a greyhound – the top speed generated on her trials was 9.61 knots.

The engines were powered by oil fuel and the crew at least was happy to be spared the mess, time and sheer physical labour of coaling. Leading Signalman Henry Mulligan wrote, '… I am glad to see we burn oil fuel … at any rate we'll coal ship through a hose.' The ship carried 45 tons of oil, which gave the ship a range of 1,440 miles when steaming at 8 knots – adequate for the sort of coastal operations demanded of her.

The engines were not reliable and were a source of constant worry to the Stokers and Engine Room Artificers responsible for their operation. Boiler trouble stopped the ship assisting in the evacuation of the Gallipoli Peninsula, and when the ship was bound for north Russia, Chief Engine Room Artificer Sydney Rutland wrote: '… we are beginning to look upon [the steering engine] as an instrument sent to blast our souls to everlasting purgatory'. The ship's design meant that the two propellers were often lifted out of the water, though Lieutenant-Commander Michell was able to correct this by adjusting the trim of the ship: 'I had extra bunkers for culinary coal built in around the small steam steering gear aft and all the ammunition stored in the aft magazine.'

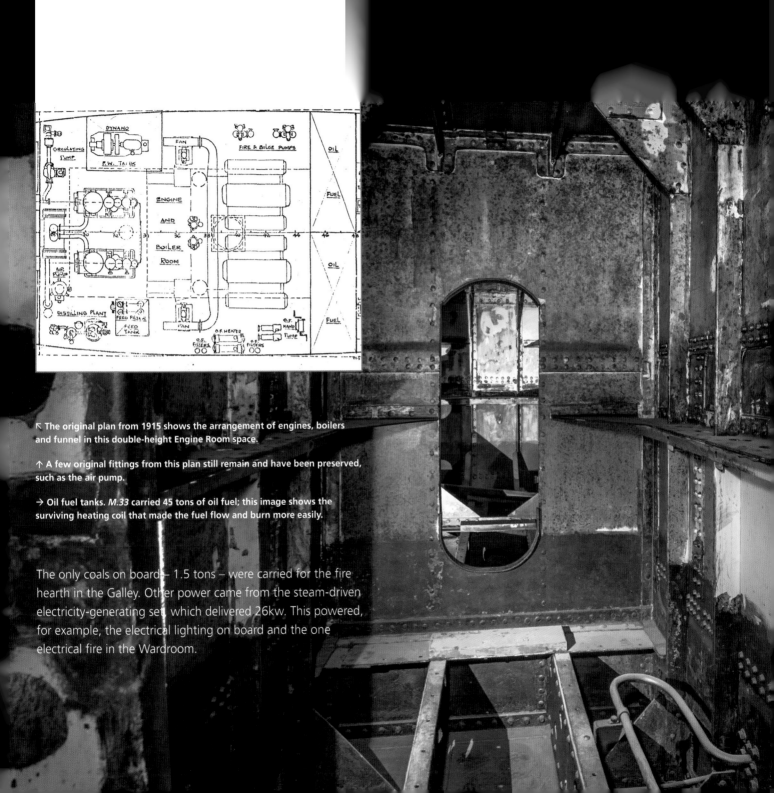

↖ The original plan from 1915 shows the arrangement of engines, boilers and funnel in this double-height Engine Room space.

↑ A few original fittings from this plan still remain and have been preserved, such as the air pump.

→ Oil fuel tanks. *M.33* carried 45 tons of oil fuel; this image shows the surviving heating coil that made the fuel flow and burn more easily.

The only coals on board – 1.5 tons – were carried for the fire hearth in the Galley. Other power came from the steam-driven electricity-generating set, which delivered 26kw. This powered, for example, the electrical lighting on board and the one electrical fire in the Wardroom.

FIGHTING *M.33*

'The firing has caused some distortion of decks and bulkheads in this ship besides a large number of minor defects such as the destruction of porcelain, electrical fittings … cabin furniture all of which can be made good by the ship's staff.'
Captain's report of proceedings, 14 August 1915

M.33's whole design was based on creating a platform for firing her main weapons – her two breech-loading 6-inch guns. The guns, mountings and ammunition weighed in at 62 tons out of a total of 580 tons. For such a small ship these were relatively powerful weapons, capable of sending a 100lb high explosive shell out to a maximum range of 14,700yds. With gun crew working at the top of their game, each gun could fire six rounds a minute, but this was notional as such rapid fire would have made accurate fire impossible.

In the gunnery trials held in June 1915 each gun fired just four rounds, so it is not surprising that when the ship went into action at Gallipoli, firing sometimes over 80 rounds a day with the guns 'red hot', there were unforeseen consequences. This firing put such a strain on the ship that all the monitors of her class were ordered to have their decks strengthened.

The barrels of the guns also had a limited life and both were replaced whilst the ship was in the Aegean: the for'ard gun in April 1917 and the aft two months later.

The Captain's reports on the ship's gunnery performance show some of the practical difficulties in accurately aiming the guns:

> The rolling of this type of vessel is so rapid that continuous laying is impossible. The period for a double roll from Port to Starboard and back again is 4.2 seconds … To overcome this difficulty the vessel is kept head to sea as much as possible and orders have been given to fire on the upward roll at shore targets and on the downward roll at submarines or other vessels.

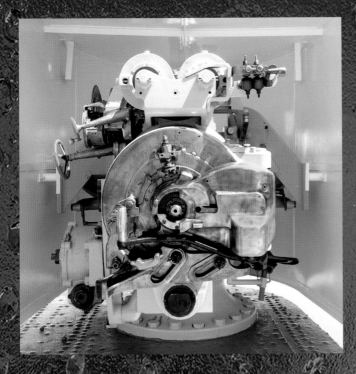

↑ The breech of the aft 6-inch gun.

↖ *M.33* could carry 200 6-inch shells in each magazine.

→ The for'ard gun. A fantastic team of museum volunteers and apprentices spent over 1,000 hours in painstaking restoration of the guns.

Since *M.33*'s guns were removed during 1924 when she was converted to a minelayer, the guns that you see today were originally mounted on other ships, but are both from the First World War. The for'ard gun was mounted on the cruiser HMS *Delhi*, and after being preserved ashore for many years at HMS *Excellent* was restored to *M.33* in 1992. The aft gun was mounted on the battleship HMS *Canada* and so was fired at the Battle of Jutland; *Canada* was sold to Chile in 1920 where the gun survived ashore until the 1990s, when the Chilean Navy generously transported it thousands of miles back to Portsmouth.

DEFENDING *M.33*

'… we were blazing away with our old 6 pounder as hard as we could'.
Diary of Leading Signalman Henry Mulligan, 29 March 1916

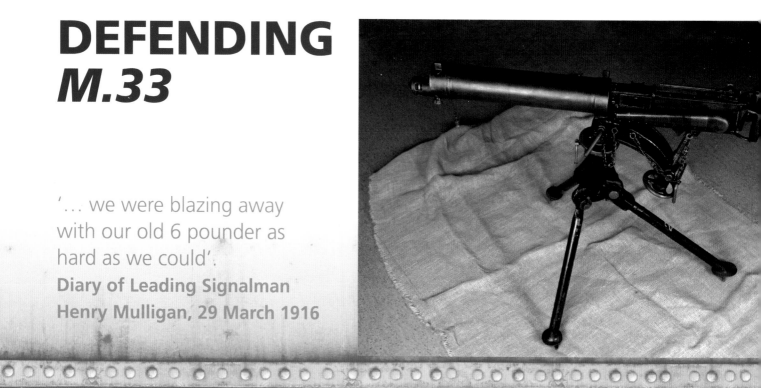

M.33 was built for attacking the shore using her main guns. For her crew it must have been worrying that she was much less well equipped for defence – indeed, that she was specifically designed to be cheap to build and relatively expendable. *M.33* had no armour to any of her hull and was too slow to run away, so action with another ship of any size was likely to be fatal.

In addition to the 6-inch guns she did have anti-aircraft guns, which were used with increasing regularity during the war against aircraft and Zeppelins. When built, this gun was a 6-pounder high-angle Hotchkiss mounted on top of the Funnel Deck, capable of firing 20 rounds a minute to a height of 8,700yds but effective to 1,200yds.

In February 1918 the Hotchkiss was replaced by a 3-inch gun. For much closer protection *M.33* carried three Maxim guns – machine guns which could be set up on either the port or starboard side and fire 450 rounds a minute. No records survive of their use during the First World War, but they are likely to have been particularly reassuring to have on the Russian rivers in 1919.

In 1918 two measures were also taken to guard against U-boat attack. The ship was fitted with a hydrophone – the new listening device trailed in the water for picking up the sound of their engines – and the crew added the distinctive dazzle paint scheme, which is seen today.

← Maxim gun. The ship had four places where these machine guns could be set up when required.

↓ The 6-pounder could fire more rapidly and at a high angle and so was *M.33*'s protection against attacking aircraft.

NAVIGATING AND COMMUNICATING

One of *M.33*'s five officers was responsible for navigation: during the Gallipoli Campaign this was Lieutenant Arthur Bowen, an experienced merchant seaman called up to serve in the Royal Naval Reserve for the duration of hostilities. At sea his place was in the Wheelhouse with the commanding officer; here one would find the chart table, engine telegraph for communicating with the Engine Room and the distinctive, raised steering platform. This position made it easy to receive bearings from the ship's compass, which was positioned on the roof, and to communicate with any seaman taking depth soundings on the Leadsmen's Platforms to port and starboard. When the ship went to north Russia the Navigating Officer sometimes went aloft to con the ship from the Crow's Nest.

This deck was also the centre for all communications between *M.33* and other ships, and the shore. Visual signals came in different forms: signal flags were hoisted on halyards up the main mast from the Compass Platform, where a semaphore also stood; the crew used portable lamps for signalling in Morse code; and just aft of the Wheelhouse, joined with a communicating hatch, was the Wireless Telegraphy Room. This little box contained *M.33*'s wireless set, which was relatively small but had a range of 50 miles.

↑ The W/T Office had wooden paneling with a felt lining – intended to insulate and provide peace and quiet for the man listening inside.

→ The Wheelhouse includes an unusual raised platform, which allowed the man steering to see over the for'ard gun.

↓ The ship's compass was set on the roof of the Wheelhouse.

A UNIQUE SURVIVOR

When *M.33* returned from Russia in October 1919 she spent four years laid up in reserve at the Nore. The fact that she avoided the fate of the other three survivors of her class – *M.29* (sold in 1946), *M.31* (broken up in 1948) and *M.32* (sold in 1920) – owes something to chance as, uniquely, the Navy found new uses for the ship (albeit ones which became less and less glamorous).

Once the Navy had no more use for *M.33*'s hull she survived just long enough to be conserved and restored by the National Museum of the Royal Navy, an act that owes much to the vision of Hampshire County Council and then of the Heritage Lottery Fund.

1919–1924	Laid up at the Nore.
1924–1925	Converted to a minelayer at Pembroke

Dockyard; re-commissioned in February 1925 and allocated to Portsmouth as a tender to the mine warfare school at HMS *Vernon* with a reduced peacetime crew of just 26.

1925–1936	Re-named HMS *Minerva* on 1 December 1925, but reduced soon afterwards to care and maintenance, occasionally re-commissioning as a tender when required.
1936	Re-commissioned as tender to HMS *Effingham*.
1939	Put up for sale in January 1939, but rescued by the start of the Second World War when she became a floating staff office.
1943	Converted to a floating boom defence workshop at White's Shipyard on the River Itchen: the engines hollowed out, mast and funnels taken down.
1944	Towed up to work on the Clyde.

← HMS *Minerva* in 1936 missing the guns which were removed in 1924.

↙ Hulk *C.23* – the final stage of the ship's service life.

↓ *M.33* came into No.1 Dock in 1997 and revealed the extent of corrosion to her hull.

1946	Returned to Portsmouth Harbour and moored at Gosport as a floating workshop and office for 25 years.
1984	Moored alongside HMS *Rhyl*, then put up for sale.
1987	Sold to the Hartlepool Ship Preservation Trust.
1990	Bought by Hampshire County Council.
1991	Towed back to the Great Basin in Portsmouth Dockyard to begin a long programme of conservation and restoration.
2014	£1.79m funding came from the Heritage Lottery Fund and the ship was transferred to the NMRN.

CONSERVATION AND RESTORATION

→ An X-ray of the paint layers on *M.33*. The preservation project has helped us to understand the paint colours applied at different stages of her life.

M.33 stayed in service for almost 70 years so the ship that survived, when Heritage Lottery Fund support made restoration possible, reflected many different parts of her career. The team working on the ship's conservation therefore faced many hard choices. For example: which parts of the ship should be restored and which left alone? Should anything original ever be removed to allow public access? Should original paintwork be re-covered? After exhaustive research, the approach taken balances conservation and restoration. Inside the hull has been preserved and stabilised, therefore the engines that were lifted out in 1943 have not been replaced. Instead, the conservation team has spent approximately 3,600 hours expertly cleaning every exposed surface by hand and coating it with Waxoyl, which acts as a preservative. This means that below decks you will see the ship in the raw, with every plate, every rivet and every layer of history exposed.

The Upper Deck has been restored, and so the guns removed in 1924, which are so important for understanding the ship's role, are now back and returned to working (if not quite firing) order by the expert volunteer team from 'Explosion! The Museum of Naval Firepower'.

Internal spaces like the cabins, Mess Deck and Wheelhouse now give an impression of how they looked in 1915, but excessive repainting has been avoided. Instead, paintwork has been kept and stabilised so visitors can be clear what is 'original' – whether that is from construction in 1915, refit in 1924 or indeed later – and what is brand new.

With this conservation-led approach, as much of the original ship has been preserved as possible, in trust that the ship will survive for another 100 years.